MW01670976

Hans Brinker and His Sister Gretel.
By Jessie Willcox Smith.

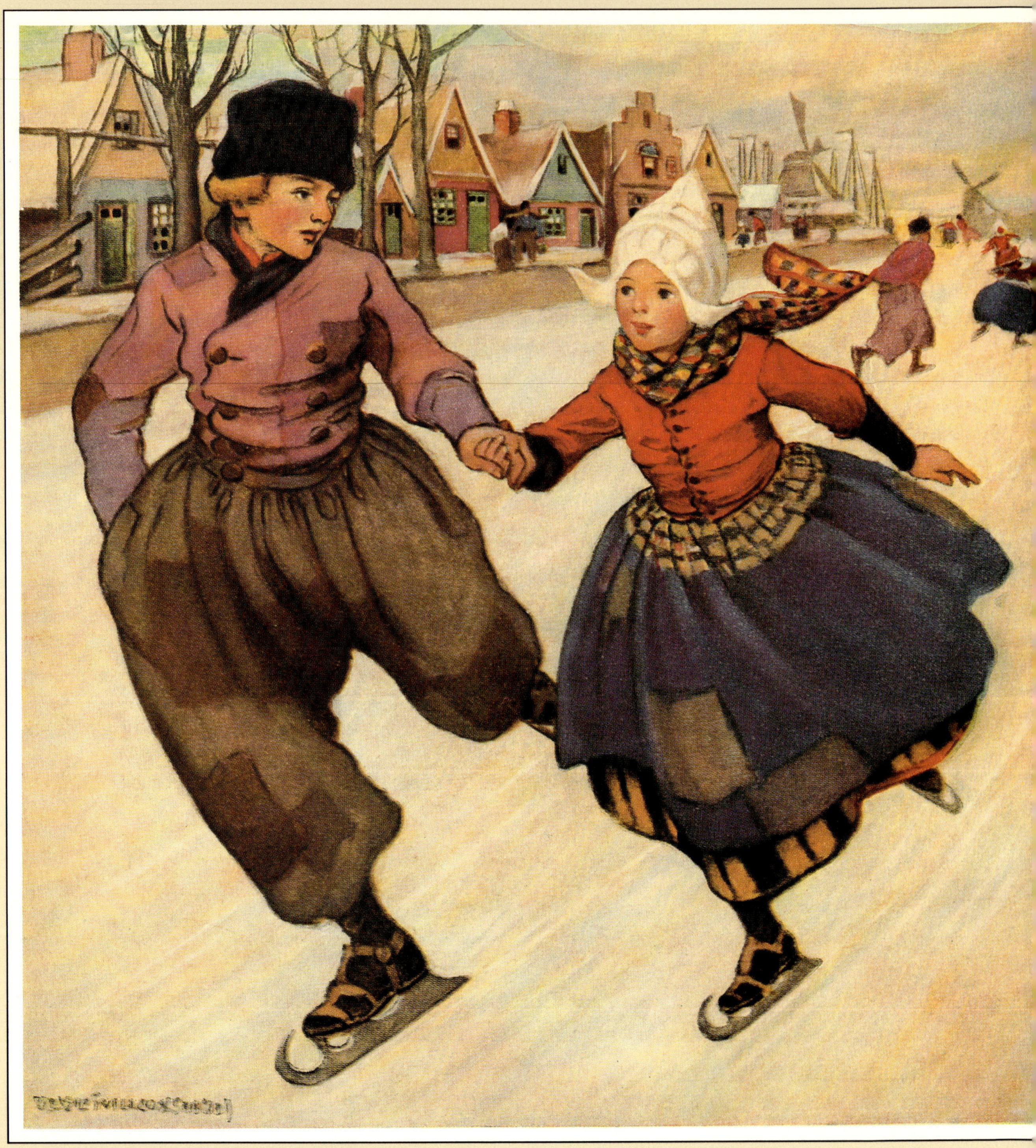

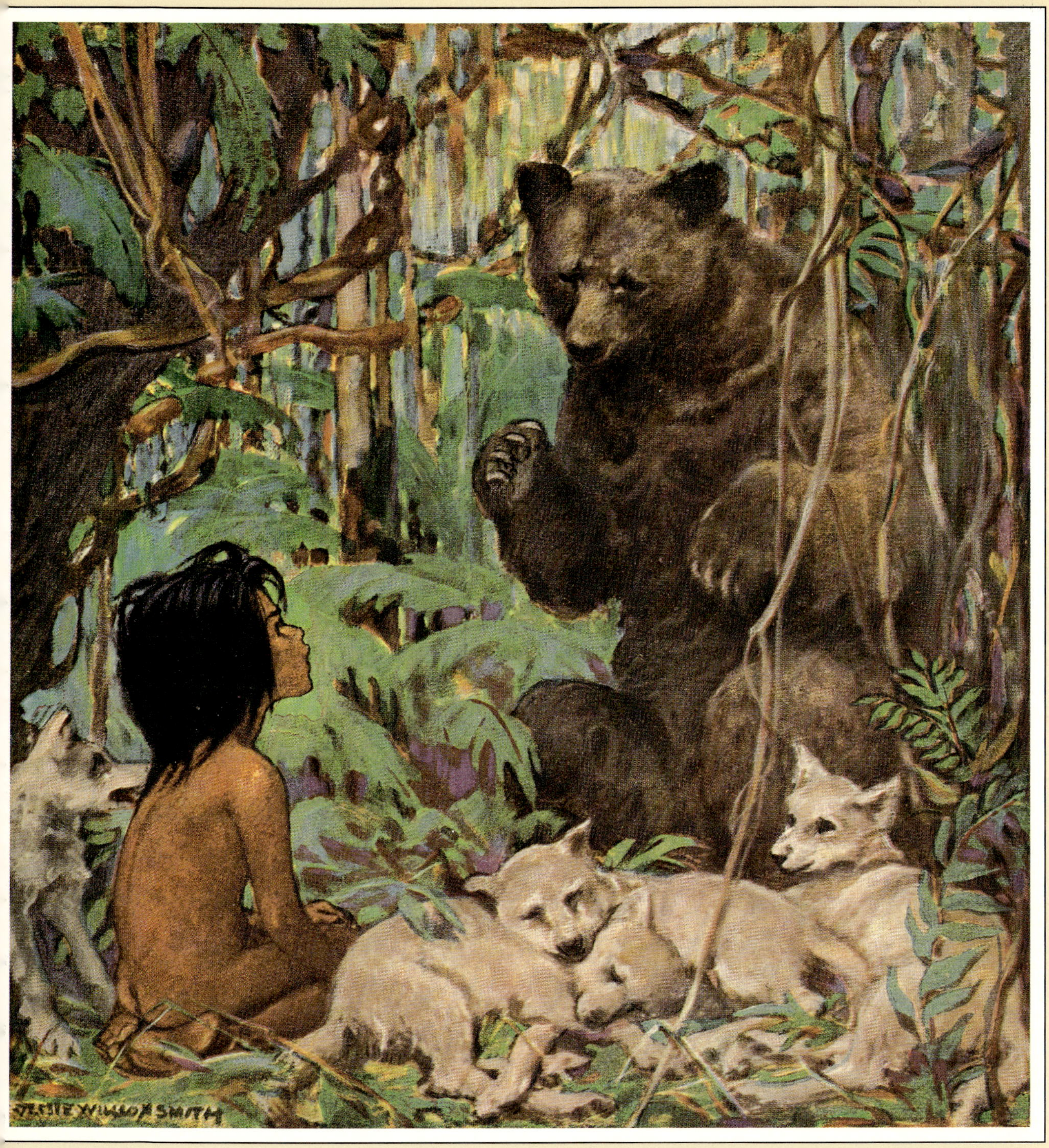
JESSIE WILLCOX SMITH

Mowgli and the Wolf Cubs Listening to Baloo.
By Jessie Willcox Smith.

Heidi with Her Goats.
By Jessie Willcox Smith.

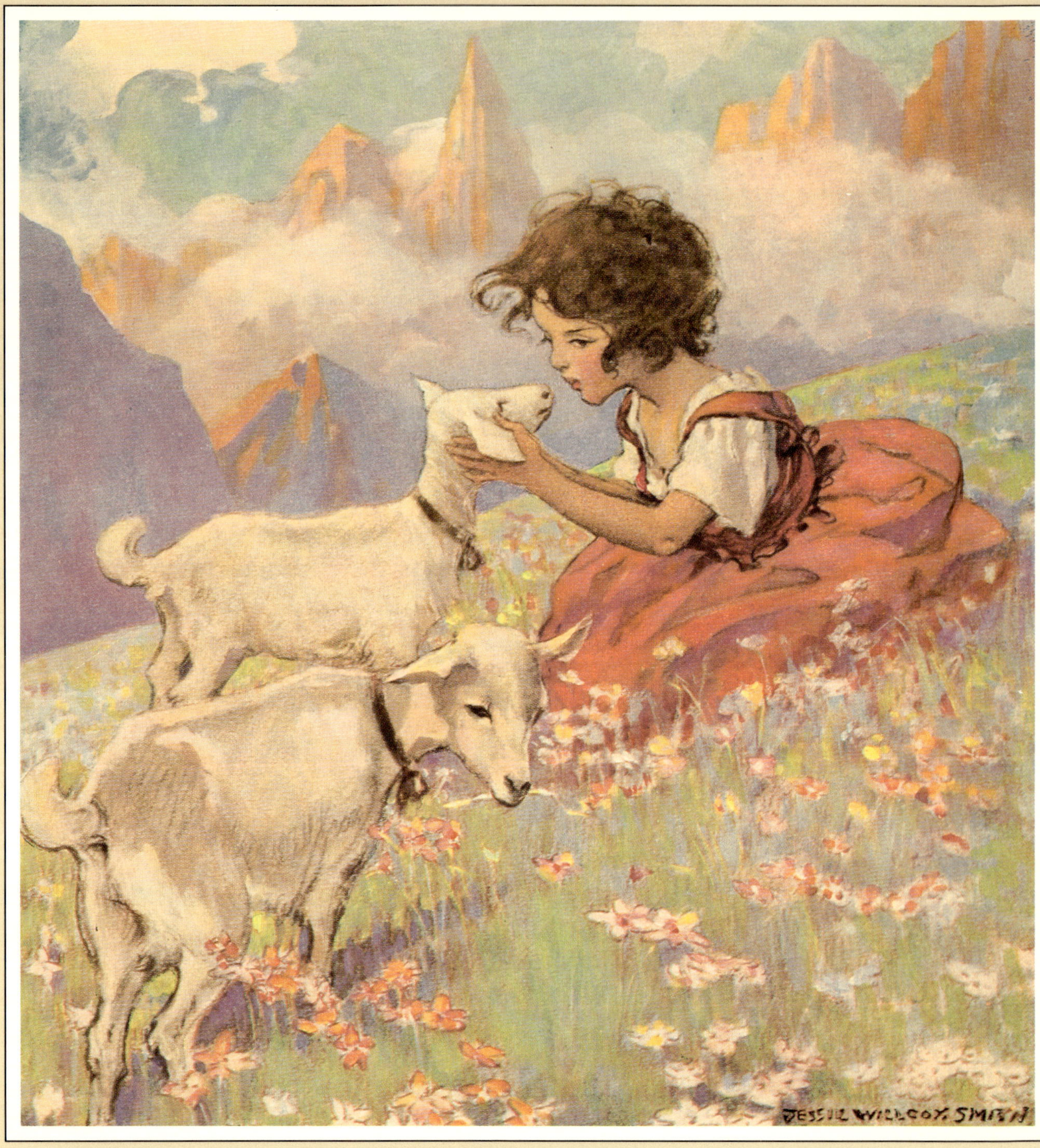
JESSIE WILLCOX SMITH

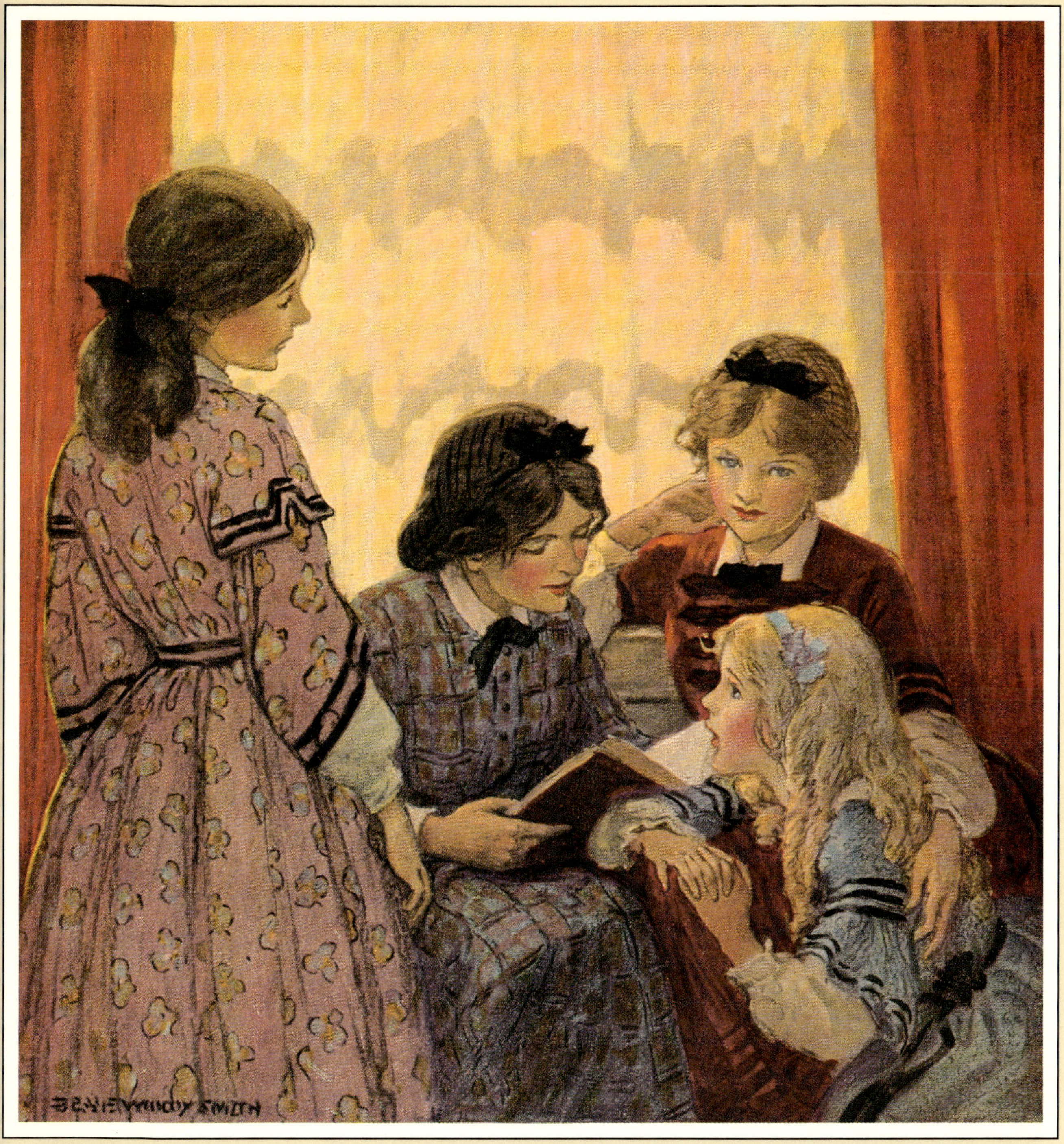

Little Women—Meg, Jo, Beth, and Amy.
By Jessie Willcox Smith.

Jackanapes.
By Jessie Willcox Smith.

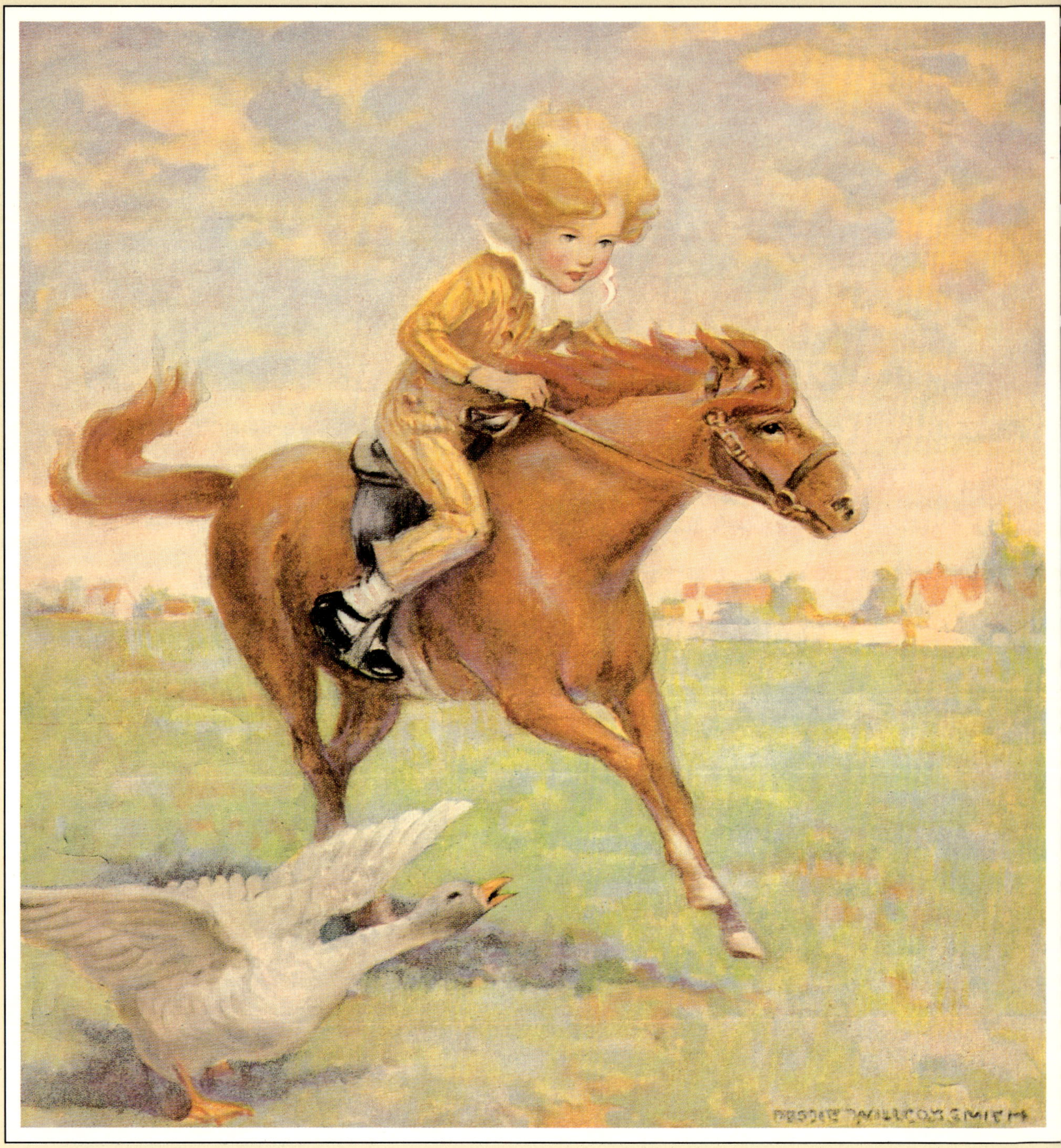

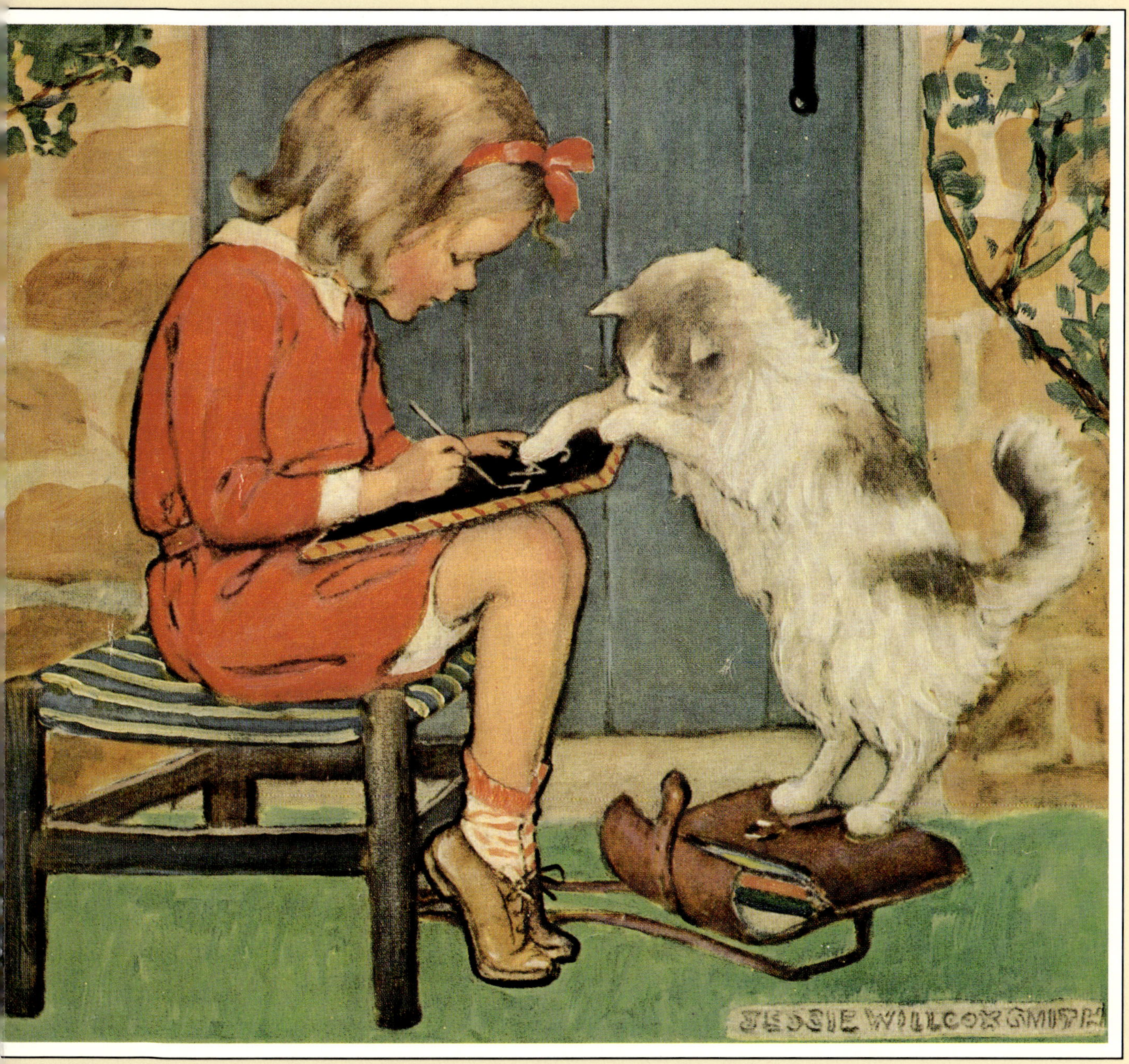
JESSIE WILLCOX SMITH

Her First Word.
By Jessie Willcox Smith.